Ragtime Gems

Original Sheet Music for 25 Ragtime Classics

Selected and with an Introduction by

David A. Jasen

Dover Publications, Inc., New York

PUBLISHER'S NOTE

Since the originals reproduced here are faithful historical documents as well as sources of enjoyment, the titles and artwork have not been changed even where they reflect the broader humor of their era, in which the nation was far less sensitive to jibes about minority groups. It is our belief that a mature understanding of our past is more fruitful than a falsification of history.

Published in Canada by General Publishing Company, Ltd., 30 Lesmill Road, Don Mills, Toronto, Ontario.

Published in the United Kingdom by Constable and Company, Ltd., 10 Orange Street, London WC2H 7EG.

Ragtime Gems: Original Sheet Music for 25 Ragtime Classics is a new collection of music, selected and with an introduction by David A. Jasen, first published by Dover Publications, Inc., in 1986. The original publishers and dates of publication of the music appear in the Contents and on the individual covers and title pages.

Manufactured in the United States of America
Dover Publications, Inc., 31 East 2nd Street, Mineola, N.Y. 11501

Library of Congress Cataloging-in-Publication Data

Ragtime gems.

For piano.
Reprint of works originally published 1904–1910.
Includes the illustrated title pages.
Contents: Dat lovin' rag / Bernard Adler
        Honey rag / Egbert Van Alstyne
        The Frisco rag / Harry Armstrong—[etc.]
1. Piano music (Ragtime)   I. Jasen, David A.
M21.R2174   1986   86-753411
ISBN 0-486-25248-5

Introduction

DAVID A. JASEN

The Golden Age of ragtime, when middle-class America not only accepted ragtime but reveled in it, lasted from 1904 to 1910. This was when ragtime was heard all over the land, especially in pleasure haunts, from the dives to the first-class vaudeville houses. It was a time when a piano was a major furnishing in most homes, and the daughter or wife of the house took lessons. It was also a time in which the sale of sheet music dominated the popular music industry and the sales of ragtime sheet music boomed. More rags were published in this period than in any other. Of course, most rags—like most other musical compositions—were either imitative of the hits or just not very good. However, those rags which caught the public's fancy tended to be snappy, toe-tapping, catchy rags with captivating themes.

This was the time when million-selling rags nearly kept pace with the million-selling songs of the time. In our day if a pop recording doesn't sell at least five million copies it is presumed to have a structural weakness. But during the first decade of this century, when the population numbered around ninety million, a piece of sheet music that couldn't be sung or danced to but nevertheless sold a million copies, had to be really something. The first genuine million-selling rag was Scott Joplin's 1899 gem, "Maple Leaf Rag" (see Dover's *Classic Piano Rags*, 20469-3), although it took nearly twenty years to achieve that sale. The next million-seller was Charles L. Johnson's 1906 favorite, and the first of the vegetable rags, "Dill Pickles" (see Jasen & Tichenor's *Rags and Ragtime, A Musical History*, for the fascinating story of how it was named). Other million-selling favorites to be found in the present volume include Jay Roberts' "Entertainer's Rag," Raymond Birch's "Powder Rag," the vaudeville team of Lyons & Yosco's delicious "Spaghetti Rag," which again proved its timelessness during the 1950's ragtime revival, Henry Lodge's "Temptation Rag," Jean Schwartz's "Whitewash Man" and Ted Snyder's "Wild Cherries." This rag was so popular and for so long that some forty years later comedian Jimmy Durante remembered vividly how he played it in the Coney Island resorts for several years.

The Scott Joplin rags included here are among his very finest; they are reprinted for the first time in a folio since the original publications: "Searchlight Rag," "Rose Leaf Rag" and his most mature masterpiece, "Fig Leaf Rag." Of special interest to the fans of James Scott will be his outstanding "Grace and Beauty," at long last in print once more. Joe Jordan's "That Teasin' Rag" has had a stormy journey since it was first published. The Original Dixieland Jazz Band used its Trio in their "Original Dixieland One-Step" recording of 1917, without bothering to get Jordan's permission. While the "One-Step" still makes for a spirited jazz number, it was originally part of this 1909 rag.

Many Tin Pan Alley song composers got their start writing rags, and we find examples galore here with Albert Gumble's "Bolo Rag," Harry Tierney's "Bumble

Bee," George Botsford's "Chatterbox Rag," Harry Armstrong's "Frisco Rag," Egbert Van Alstyne's "Honey Rag" and Herbert Ingraham's "Poison Ivy."

The earliest rag here is New Orleanian Al Verges' "Whoa! You Heiffer," extraordinarily scarce as a piece of sheet music today, although it was recorded on both discs and piano rolls in 1904 and achieved wide popularity. Another New Orleans rag, Bob Hoffman's "I'm Alabama Bound," was used in many songs by various composers. One of these, fellow-New Orleanian Jelly Roll Morton, pretty much made it his property.

The Midwest's contribution to ragtime has not been ignored, and is represented here by Bernie Adler's "Dat Lovin' Rag," Frank Henri Klickmann's "Knockout Drops" and J. Russel Robinson's "Sapho Rag." New York City boasts three orchestra leaders turned ragtime composers: Malvin Franklin and Arthur Lange, co-writers of the winter drink favorite, "Hot Chocolate Rag," and Ford T. Dabney, composer of "Oh! You Devil" (a couple of years later, he repented when he wrote "Oh! You Angel!").

The sounds of ragtime are as varied as the performers who play them. The feelings engendered by these rags are equally varied, but uppermost are the gaiety and high spirits that abound on each page. These rags represent America at its playful best.

Contents

Publisher, city and date are in parentheses.

That Lovin' Rag.
Two Step.

By SMALLEY & ADLER.

Moderato.

Bernard Adler

THE FRISCO RAG

BY

HARRY ARMSTRONG

COMPOSER OF
"I LOVE MY WIFE, BUT OH YOU KID"
"BABY DOLL" "SWEET ADELINE"
"CAN'T YOU SEE I'M LONELY" ETC

Instrumental

M. WITMARK & SONS
New York   Chicago   San Francisco
London   Paris

Respectfully dedicated to Mr. John Morrisey Mgr. Orpheum Theatre San Fr. Cal.

The Frisco Rag.

HARRY ARMSTRONG.

Moderato. *(Play very slow.)*

The Frisco Rag

Harry Armstrong

POWDER RAG

by Raymond Birch

COMPOSER OF "ALL THE MONEY"

PUBLISHED BY

Chas. L. Johnson & Co.

KANSAS CITY, MO.

"Powder Rag"
March and Two-Step

RAYMOND BIRCH
Composer of
"All the Money"

TRIO

Raymond Birch

Chatterbox Rag

By George Botsford

POPULAR EDITION

JEROME H. REMICK & Co. ~ New York ~ Detroit

Chatterbox Rag

GEORGE BOTSFORD

Not fast

George Botsford

Chatterbox Rag

George Botsford

OH! YOU DEVIL
RAG

Composed by
FORD T. DABNEY

As
Introduced
by
AIDA
OVERTON
WALKER
America's
Foremost
Colored
Comedienne

6

Published by "Shapiro" MUSIC PUBLISHER
Cor Broadway & Thirty Ninth Street
New York.

STARMER

"OH, YOU DEVIL"
Rag.

Moderato.

By FORD T. DABNEY.

20

Trio.

Ford T. Dabney

CODA.

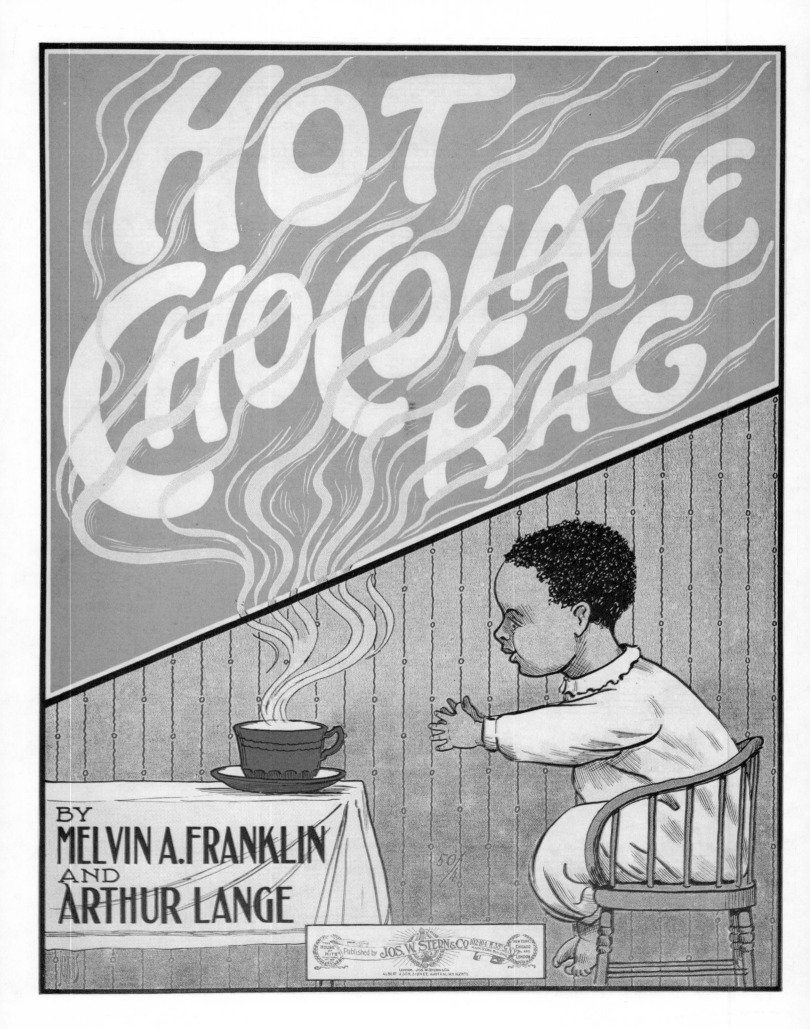

Hot Chocolate.
Rag.

by Malvin Franklin and
Arthur Lange.

Franklin & Lange

THE BOLO RAG

by

Albert Gumble

5

Jerome H. Remick & Co. New York Detroit

STARMER

The "Bolo" Rag

Tempo di Rago
slowly but surely

ALBERT GUMBLE

Albert Gumble

The Bolo Rag

Albert Gumble

I'm Alabama Bound.

By ROBT. HOFFMAN.

34

Marcato il canto.

Robert Hoffman

H. A. Bettinger

POISON IVY

RAG

COMPOSED BY

HERBERT INGRAHAM

5

Published by "Shapiro" MUSIC PUBLISHER

- Cor Broadway & Thirty Ninth Street. New York.

STARMER

Poison Ivy!

RAG.

Tempo di Marcia.

By HERBERT INGRAHAM.

TRIO.

Herbert Ingraham

"DILL PICKLES"

(TWO STEP.)

CHARLES L. JOHNSON.

Dill Pickles

TRIO.

Charles L. Johnson

Dill Pickles

"FIG LEAF"
A High Class Rag.

NOTE.- Do not play this piece fast. It is never right to play "Ragtime" fast. Composer

By SCOTT JOPLIN
Composer of "Maple Leaf Rag"

Fig Leaf Rag

Scott Joplin

COMPANION TO **MAPLE LEAF RAG** BY SAME COMPOSER.

ROSE LEAF RAG

A RAGTIME TWO-STEP

— BY —

SCOTT JOPLIN

COMPOSER OF "CASCADES" "SUNFLOWER SLOW DRAG" ETC.

PUBLISHED BY
JOS. M. DALY MUSIC CO.
BOSTON, MASS.

5

ROSE LEAF RAG.

A Ragtime Two Step.

NOTE :— Do not play this piece fast
It is never right to play "Ragtime" fast.
Composer.

By SCOTT JOPLIN
Composer of "Maple Leaf Rag."

Slow March tempo

Piano.

Scott Joplin

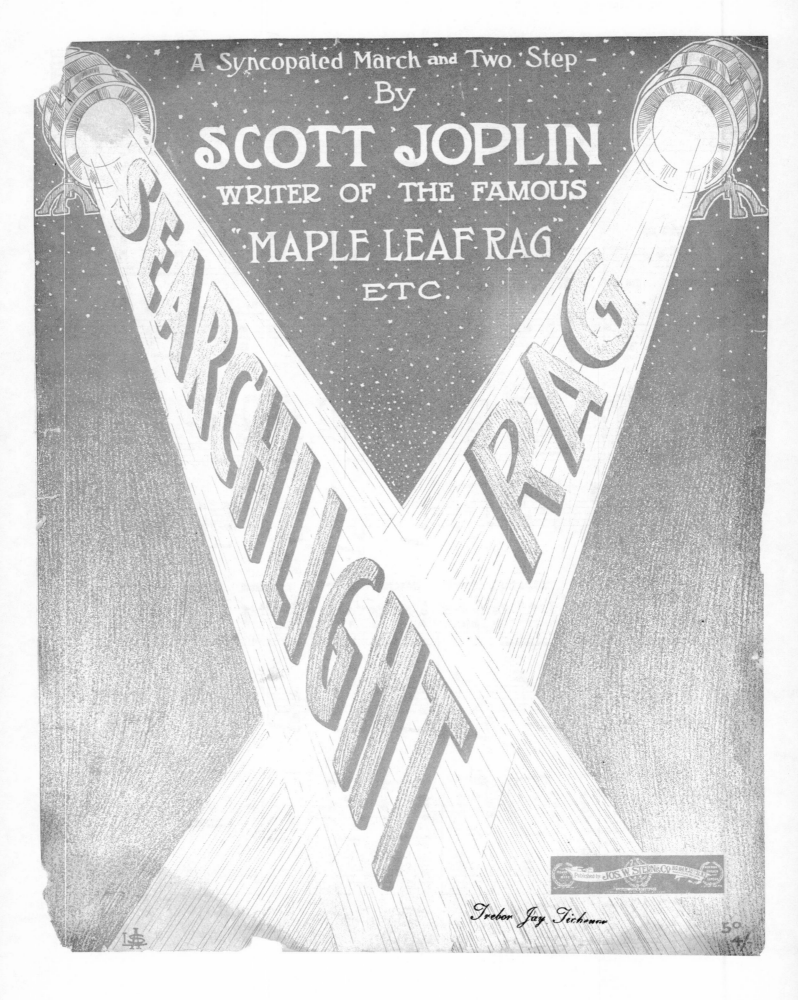

"Search-Light Rag."

Notice: Do not play this piece fast.
It is never right to play "Ragtime" fast.
Composer.

By SCOTT JOPLIN.
Composer of "Maple Leaf Rag," etc.

Scott Joplin

THAT TEASIN' RAG

WORDS & MUSIC BY
JOE JORDAN

INSTRUMENTAL

Published for

Vocal	50c.
Vocal (Simplified)	50c.
Instrumental	50c.
Small Orchestra	75c.
Full Orchestra	1.15
Full Band	50c.

THE MOST POPULAR "RAG" Success of the Day

Featured by

Girls from Happyland Company

A TERRIFIC HIT WITH

EDDIE LEONARD

Published by JOS. W. STERN & CO. 102-104 W 38 ST N
NEW YORK CHICAGO LONDON

That Teasin' Rag.
Rag Two Step.

By JOE JORDAN.
arranged by Wm. H. Tyers.

Moderato.

Joe Jordan

D. C.

KNOCKOUT DROPS

RAG

BY
F. HENRI KLICKMANN

5

CARL LAEMMLE MUSIC COMPANY
CHICAGO   NEW YORK

KNOCK-OUT DROPS.
RAG.

Tempo di Rag. *Not too fast.*

F. HENRI KLICKMANN

F. Henri Klickmann

Knockout Drops

F. Henri Klickmann

Temptation Rag

Two-Step

By

Henry Lodge

50¢
2½ NET

M. Witmark & Sons.
New York Chicago London Paris

Temptation Rag.

Allegretto con moto. M. M. ♩ = 108.

HENRY LODGE.

Temptation Rag

Henry Lodge

SPAGHETTI RAG

RESTORANTI

COMPOSED, PLAYED
AND
INTRODUCED BY

LYONS & YOSCO

Published by "Shapiro" MUSIC PUBLISHER
Cor Broadway & Thirty Ninth Street
New York.

6

Spaghetti Rag.

Slowly.

LYONS & JOSCO.

Sempre Moderato

Lyons & Yosco

THE ENTERTAINER'S RAG

⑥

BY
JAY
ROBERTS

FEATURED BY — LLOYD & ROBERTS.

Pacific Coast Music Co.
Music Publishers,
Oakland, Cal.

The Entertainer's Rag

By JAY ROBERTS

✻Moderato (not too fast)

Jay Roberts

Jay Roberts

SAPHO RAG

5

By
J. Russell Robinson

PUBLISHERS OF
RAG TIME THAT IS DIFFERENT
STARK MUSIC CO.
ST. LOUIS, MO.   127 EAST 23 ST   NEW YORK

Trebor Jay Tichenor

"SAPHO RAG."

Introduction.
Moderato.

J. RUSSEL ROBINSON.

Sapho Rag

TRIO.

J. Russel Robinson

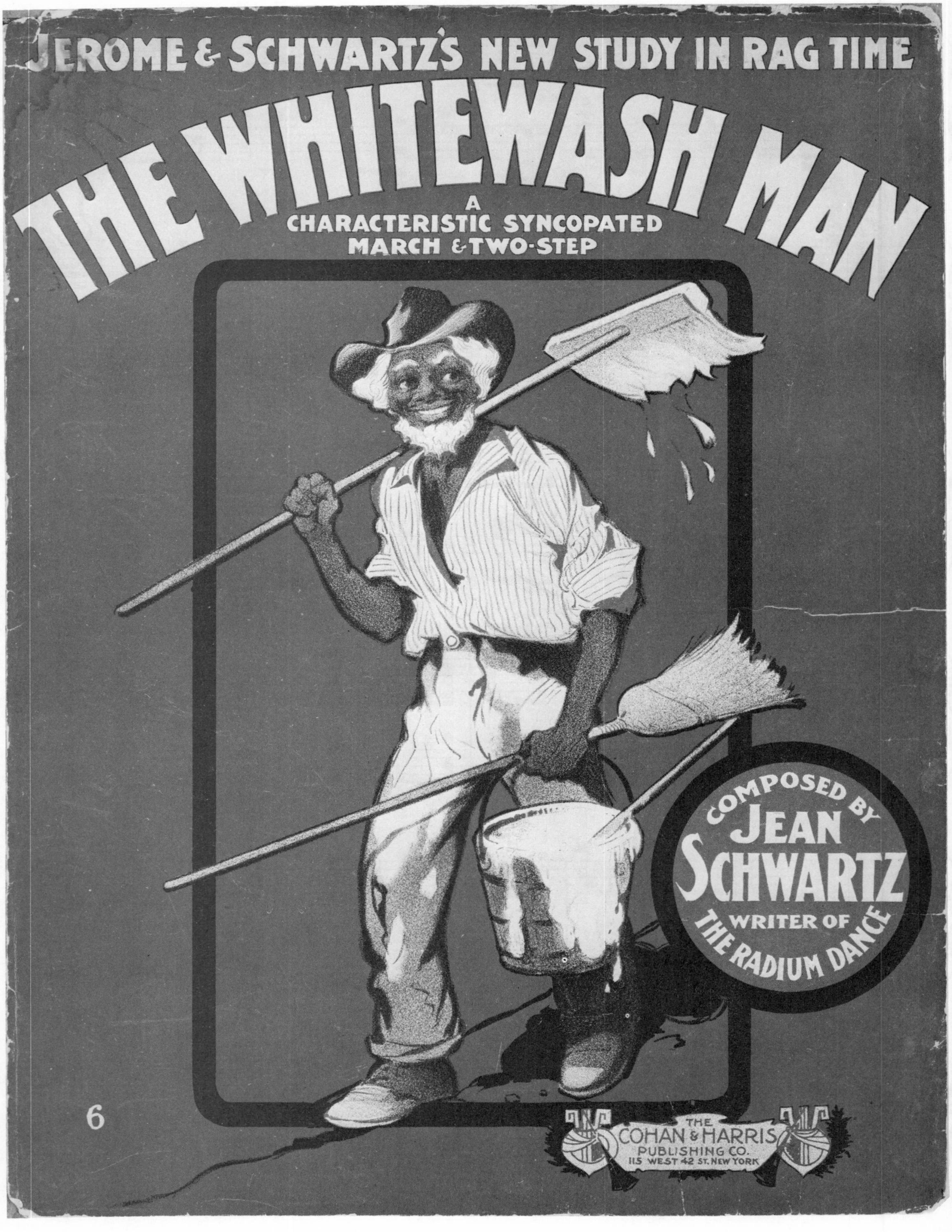
JEROME & SCHWARTZ'S NEW STUDY IN RAG TIME
THE WHITEWASH MAN
A
CHARACTERISTIC SYNCOPATED
MARCH & TWO-STEP
COMPOSED BY
JEAN
SCHWARTZ
WRITER OF
THE RADIUM DANCE
6
THE
COHAN & HARRIS
PUBLISHING CO.
115 WEST 42 ST. NEW YORK

THE WHITE WASH MAN

BY JEAN SCHWARTZ.

Tempo di Rag.

92

TRIO.

94

GRACE AND BEAUTY.

(a classy Rag.)

N.B. Do not play this piece fast,
Composer.

JAMES SCOTT.

Grace and Beauty

TRIO.

James Scott

WILD CHERRIES

Characteristique RAG

AMY BUTLER

by

TED SNYDER

TED SNYDER Co.
MUSIC PUBLISHERS
112 WEST 38 St. NEW YORK.

Wild Cherries
Rag.

By TED SNYDER

Tempo di Marcia

Ted Snyder

Trio

Ted Snyder

BUMBLE BEE RAG.

(A BUZZING RAG)

HARRY A. TIERNEY

Harry A. Tierney

The Bumble Bee

Harry A. Tierney

HONEY RAG
HONEY
BY
EGBERT VAN ALSTYNE
5
JEROME H. REMICK & Co ~ New York ~ Detroit

HONEY RAG.

TWO-STEP.

EGBERT Van ALSTYNE.

Egbert Van Alstyne

COW-BOY INTERMEZZO.

WHOA! YOU HEIFFER

A WARM RAG

BY AL. VERGES.

PUBLISHED BY HAKENJOS Pub. Co. NEW ORLEANS

F. J. A. FORSTER,
Chicago Ill.
51

Whoa You Heiffer.

AL. VERGES.

Whoa you Heif - fer

Al Verges

Al Verges